WORDS

FROM THE HEART

A
REFLECTION
IN POETRY

Sister Magdala Marie Gilbert, OSP

WORDS
FROM THE HEART

A Reflection in Poetry

Sister Magdala Marie Gilbert, OSP

Order this book online at www.trafford.com
or email orders@trafford.com

Most Trafford titles are also available at major online book retailers.

Printed in the United States of America.

ART: Allegany Art
    2924 W. Curtis Street
    Tampa, FL 33614
Generic—general art:

ISBN: 978-1-4269-9753-2 (sc)
ISBN: 978-1-4269-9754-9 (e)

Trafford rev. 10/05/2011

 www.trafford.com

North America & international
toll-free: 1 888 232 4444 (USA & Canada)
phone: 250 383 6864 ♦ fax: 812 355 4082

Contents

ACKNOWLEDGEMENT

Special thanks to my family and those people in my life who had such great faith in me. Special thanks to Sr. Elaine Frederick, OSP for editing this book of poetry.

PREFACE

Writing poetry, for me is a wonderful release of energy. It eases stress and connects me with that inner peace which builds tranquility of spirit. Writing is not so much about words but using words to formulate energy to speak to the soul and keep one in one's essence.

May all who read these pages find a poem that lifts their spirit, make them laugh or make them pause and reflect.

I thank God and the Holy Spirit for giving me the ability to pen my thoughts in poetry. Some write journals, I chose to write my journal through the art of poetry.

Wisdom

(Blank Verse)

Wisdom
can be possessed
by anyone
who has faith in God,
a firm belief
in providence
and
deep trust.

Wisdom
is not afforded
only to the
elderly.

Give God Glory

(Free Verse)

Glorify
the Lord
every moment
of every day.

Praise
God in every way.

Thank
the Lord
for graces
and blessings
sent our
way.

We Christians

(Free Verse)

Many of us call ourselves Christians,
Yet when elections come we wonder.
People of integrity, or so we believed
Do some strange and irrational blunders.

Some will lie and tarnish another
We say things that mislead others.
Foes become friends for Party sake,
But really cannot tolerate the sister or brother.

Most will do and condone anything,
Just to obtain that single vote or two.
Haters come out of hiding expressing,
How they really feel about others view.

There must be a better way
To gain votes for one's Party sheet,
Without character assassination
Putting others dirty linens in the street.

All know what the Good Book says
That everyone is equal in God's sight.
A good campaign is possible with clean thoughts
If God is to be in the mix, all must be done right.

Rage

(Adage)

Rage to rage . . .
That's what they call mad,
Your mind has left.
You think you are daft
And maybe you are!

Allegany Arts

Intrigue

(Adage)

Spiritual intrigue mystifies the common person
who is no seeker of deep truth.
Where one divulges into the mystery
of the ancient who sought solace
in the desert of silence.

Allegany Arts

God's Essence

(Blank Verse)

God, you are the essence
of all life,
without your constant vigilance
we cease to be;
all would revert to nothing
without you.

Your power invigorates
all life forms . . .
in the celestial sphere,
on earth and under the earth
Nothing would exist
without your providential care.

Having Your Way

(Katauta)

Selfishness is bad.
People will shun you for sure
if your actions are not pure.

No one is perfect
but manners must be gracious
since to God we are precious.

Allegany Arts

Grow Not Weary

(Senryu)

When we grow weary
of this journey in this life,
look to our Anchor.

God will be our strength,
our rampart and our bulwark,
trust only in Him.

We can count on God
to be there in times of trials,
trust Him at all times.

So grow not weary
of tribulations and stress,
God is our stronghold.

If in Need

(Free Verse)

If you need something,
would you ask?
Or would you take
someone
immediately to task?
For your want of a meaningful call
refusing to bend
with such gall?

Allegany Arts

In Crisis

(Senryu)

Earth is in crisis
individuals must help
or we'll all perish.

Crises in our air
crisis in our water-ways
crisis with glaciers.

Cannot tiptoe now
as if the world is pristine
we all know the facts.

Allegany Arts

Politicians

(Sonnet)

Some might think politics is where it's at.
Many look for prestige and instant fame
but there really is more to it than that
politics is serious . . . it's no game.

They will be working for the common good
many lives and countries are all at stake.
One must be above-board not in the hood
you have to be honest for your own sake.

Cheating and game-playing is not so cool
God is not pleased if on greed they should feed
One will pay dearly for being a fool.
Politicians must sow good sturdy seeds.

All should pray for the persons who would then
run for any nomination and win.

Sometimes We Rebel

(Couplet)

Sometimes we rebel and sin,
thinking we can always win.

God sometimes allows a fall
so that we can heed his call.

We are always welcomed back
when we falter from lack of tack.

Our God truly loves us all
He wants to prevent our fall.

By talking to God each day,
makes us see things in His way.

Watchers

(Adage)

Watchers of stars looked patiently
to the heavens
at Northern Lights, moon changes
and elsewhere beyond the planets.

Allegany Arts

Life is Pushy

(Rondelet)

Life is pushy
prodding you to achieve greatness.
Life is pushy
as you steadily resist change
but to bloom, old habits must go
so that the new habits can grow.
Life is pushy.

Life is pushy
as emerging strength dominates.
Life is pushy
when the ego is quite ready
to embrace and own what is new
through observation as it grew.
Life is pushy.

Procrastination

(Katauta)

Procrastination
steals our time away daily,
when we tarry with our chores.

We cannot retrieve
wasted time and energy,
we pay for time that is wasted.

We have to account
for any time we squander
here or in eternity.

Calming Clouds

(Free Verse)

Calming clouds hover above as cars zoom by.
Folks never remember to look up at the clear blue sky
Minds on things to be done or left undone
Never giving thought to the dome up above.

God sees us as we zip to our destinations,
Smiles as we think of our own intentions.
But loves us all as blue sky looms above
Protecting us from harmful rays of the sun.

The Invisible

(Blank Verse)

Why do you look at me as if I am not here?
My face you look upon but do not see.
I am the poor beggar on the street corner
I am the prostitute with no one to love.

I am the project kids living in rat infested homes.
I am the drug addict on the street corner
I am the immigrant who needs a job
I am the homeless family evicted to the streets.

I am that person you cross the street to avoid.
I AM THE INVISIBLE . . .
Loved by God just like you and you and you.
I AM THE INVISIBLE . . .

Look at me, really, really look at me . . . .
Created by the same God . . .
with a soul full of His Spirit . . . Look at me
THE INVISIBLE . . . and love me.

What One Thing?

(Free Verse)

What one thing makes the love in you rise?
The innocence seen in a little child's eyes
while holding her close to your heart,
thanking God for this wonderful work of art.

What does innocence mean to you?

A challenge from the World of Poets.

Allegany Arts

God Will Never Forget

(Free Verse)

Because God is our parent
as parent, will never forget us,
will love us even when we do fuss
no matter how egregious our faults.

A good parent never hold grudges
and will not allow us to perish
but is still there to cherish
and there always to nudge us.

No parent will allow a child to suffer,
the parent is there to console
and sometimes to scold
when sick or in deep trouble.

When the child rebels and strays
the parent is also there to hold
the child even after the child was so bold
as to run away from home.

Our parent will never forsake us,
even when we do not love ourselves,
God's love is always there to caress
and holds us in a warm embrace.

In the Bayou

(Sonnet)

In the bayou of Louisiana,
alligators roam freely and are kings
basking in the warm sun in their manner
showing all that their reign is the main thing.

Life is not safe in their territory
they rule with an iron fist in this land.
Creatures of the swamp have their own story
about these bullies and their upper hand.

Despite the terror in these marshy swamps,
beauty thrives in this land so dangerous.
Beautiful cranes live and animals romp
Life is sweet but can be precarious.

Do not allow fear to dominate life,
even animals are not free from strife.

Allegany Arts

Hiding is Useless

(Blank Verse)

Lord, you are all knowing
To hide from you is useless,
To you, we are as a pane of glass.
Knowing our every thought,
Before we even think the idea.
You know the whole of it.

You who created the heavens
And all it contains . . . .
The seas, rivers and flowing streams.
The birds, insect and all the animals, too,
Mountains, valleys and sloping slopes
All these bow down to you.

We give you our true homage
Seeking to be of one accord and contentment,
Living in peace with our sisters and brothers.
Nationality does not matter at all
All are made from the same fabric . . . dirt.
With you as our parent forever.

So to hide from you is useless
For you O God know us, every one
Through and through from dirt to dirt.

Based on Psalm 139.

Nature Absorbs Us

(Senryu)

Nature absorbs us,
Our imaginations peak
At its mystery.

Changing fashion each year
Filling earth's residence
With so much joy.

Winter, summer, spring and fall
Continue to fascinate us
No matter the age.

Allegany Arts

Praise the Lord

(Free Verse)

Praise the Lord for skies so blue and so fair
with fluffy white cumulus clouds so rare
hovering over earth of fresh plowed field.

Tall bright red barns dotted the yard so green
animals graced the bustling barn yard scene.
The sight is too marvelous to behold.

Creation is here for our enjoyment
Every blade of grass, tree and river was meant
to make us see the work of the Creator.

The Lord gives us all this for our pleasure
We must honor and cherish this treasure.
You, O Lord, are wonderful . . . we praise you.

Walking on the Beach

(Senryu)

Walking on the beach
meditating with my Lord
totally in sync.

Walking hand in hand,
God talks to me . . . I listen,
my soul is joyful.

Allegany Arts

Don't Quit

(Nonet)

When life is burdensome and all seems lost
~ go to that quiet place inside ~
~ that is always there to help ~.
It's the voice that says peace
be still for I'm here.
It's God speaking
to your heart
to come
rest.

Grace of Discernment

(Free Verse)

The Lord gave me the grace of discernment,
To differentiate what is right, God's way.
So discernment could show me Satan's wiles,
As this journey of life unfolds each day.

I asked God to take me out of the way,
Keeping me humble so that I can grow.
And allow me the strength to empty me
So that His divine will I'll always know.

Images

(Free Verse)

God sends us various images in life
Important ones and not so important.
Our job is to determine which are right . . .
Which deter our union in an instant.

This can be people or it may be things.
Images are choices that we make each day,
Which affect our relationship with God
As we try to walk the straight path, God's way.

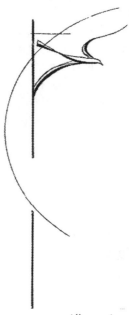

Allegany Arts

Memories

(Blank Verse)

Memories
are ways to connect
to the past.
Remembrance
about good and not so good
events in our lives.

Nonetheless
life would not be life
if all was
so perfect
without some clouds in our path
to make us grateful.

Memories
are what gets us through
our sorrows,
sparks our joy
gives us strength to carry on
in spite of life's turns.

One Dozen Roses

(Senryu)

One dozen roses
magnificent to behold
giving someone love.

It does not take much
to show love and affection
to one we hold dear.

Allegany Arts

New Year Reflections

(Blank Verse)

How can one properly thank God?
In ways that are fitting,
Because God is God . . . and
There is no other as good as God.

Yet God wants us to be thankful.
Not from a sense of guilt,
Because God is God . . . and
There is no other as good as God.

God loves you, all the world, and me
For God is our friend in need and deed.
Because God is God . . . and
There is no other as good as God.

Each New Year we thank God,
We thank God for another year of living,
For another year to praise and give thanks.
Because God is God . . . and
There is no other as good as God.

Thank you God, the God of New Years,
The God of New Years long past and yet to come.
Because God is God . . . and
There is no other as good as God.

Ministry

(Dodoitsu)

Ministry is important
In the life of the Christian.
Focus must remain on God
If God is to reign.

All glory belongs to God
Who gives strength to those who ask.
We must not hinder God's work,
We are means . . . not ends.

Flying High

(Free Verse)

Flying high in the murky sky
Houses looking like doll houses with maids
Played in by little girls in braids.

Flying high amid fluffy clouds
Looking like icing on a birthday cake
Twisting into different shapes it takes.

Flying high in the lofty sky
We can almost touch the heavens
Where the Angels fly freer than ever.

Flying high in the blue sky
God seems closer than ever
Giving you a goose-pimply shiver.

Higher and higher we fly
Into the heavenly realm
Where God is at the helm.

Good and Evil

(Free Verse)

Good always follow evil's might
As day follows the dark night
Evil cannot prevail in God's sight
God will deliver us from Satan's plight.

Allegany Arts

In Tune with God

(Free Verse)

If we are always in tune with God
We have no time to be vindictive or mean.
We can serve God with a mind that's clean.

A mean-spirited person will not grow
In the love and holiness that is owed God
Our creator who loves us and spares the rod.

All persons are called to personal holiness
And by example lead others to holiness, too
That means all are to be Saints . . . yes, me and you.

Memorial Day

(Free Verse)

A day we remember our heroes
A reminder that freedom is not cheap
That it comes from sweat and blood
That causes us to mourn and to weep.

These precious lives for freedom given
In land and seas far, far away
Our daughters and sons do their lives give
Fighting so bravely in lands so far away.

So let not their valiant deeds be for naught
As we sing their praises and remember deed
Unselfishly done without thought of pay or praise
It's just a duty one does for ones country . . . for free.

We pray for the war in Iraq and other places
Like Afghanistan, where the Taliban's thrive
Where we have to hunt Ben Laden
And bring him to justice for that infamous 9/11 day.

Memorial Day we have to honor too
Our veterans of long ago . . . those who fought
In world wars I and II keeping in mind
Korea and that Vietnam War too.

This day we thank God for such brave souls
Who continue to fight so valiantly for our freedom
Fighting on land, sea and sky
For you and for me . . . let us be grateful.

The New Year

(Blank Verse)

The New Year comes and then it goes
The only thing is . . .
We wish we could keep it longer.

The year comes and the year goes.

Just like the thief of tides
We wish we could bottle it up
So we could cherish it more.

The year comes and the year goes.

But memories are all we have
To hang on to from year to year
Fond memories of graces and blessings.

The year comes and the year goes.

Memories of sadness and of joy
Etched in our consciousness to cherish
Long after the year has past.

The year comes and the year goes.

Warm Embrace

(Free Verse)

Your warm embrace led us to you, Jesus
When Satan had us earthly bound un-free
Caves of fire cannot consume us
If when assailed by evil we turn to thee.

You are the healer of wounds
Inflicted in our fight against the evil one
Evil that hounds our every step
Trying to entrap us all to sin . . . just for fun!

Satan cannot hope to prevail
 Against Jesus who has triumphed for you and me
Over all the wiles and taunts of the devil
Dying for us at Calvary on a wretched tree.

Rejection

(Senryu)

Rejection's so cold
It can kill the very soul
And put out your fire.

It's like hell, I'm told
But was not sold until my
soul it did so sear.

Friends look at you strange
You think you're a bit deranged
Rug is pulled from feet.

Jesus was mocked too
Feels your pain when done to you
So cling to Jesus.

He'll . . . never reject
But will guard and protect you
Live for him alone.

Rejection's so cold.

Words Can Heal

(Anaphora)

Words can be very healing
Words too can be very harsh
Words can be so appealing.

Words can spearhead ambition
Words can lift one to greatness
Words may lead to contrition.

Let not unkind words leave you
Let others live timid free
Let your words speak of love too.

Let words not ruin others lives
Let all try the Golden Rule
Let us try nice words to give.

Searing words can kill the soul
Searing words leave lasting scars
Searing words leave a deep hole.

Think before you speak so bold
Think of the soul you will sear
Think . . . practice the tongue to hold.

(Seven syllable count each line.)

The Road Ahead

(Free Verse)

There I stood with hands on hips
Pretending to look in the distance for ships
From this distance the road resembles water
Waiting for ships to stay and to barter.

Maybe I'll wander up that way
I really don't want to linger or stay
I just want to see what's over there
It might be fun, though it looks so far.

Maybe I'll venture out when Mom is near
So that I won't have no fear
But what a beautiful sight
Sun making everything looks so bright.

Blue sky meeting gray earth and all
Making me look so very small
Thinking and pondering
With hands on hips . . . wondering.

=============+===========

Written from observing a photo of a child standing with her hands on her hips in the middle of the road. A Challenge from A World of Poets site.

Sitting by the Sea

(Limerick)

Sitting on the calm shore of the sea
A boy looked out for a ship to see
Along came a big cat
Chasing a big fat rat
Cat chased rat along shore of the sea.

Allegany Arts

I Prayed the Rosary Today

(Free Verse)

I prayed the Rosary today,
for all the ills in this world
that peace will reign all over
especially in Iraq and Afghanistan.

I prayed the rosary today
for aborted babies from rejected wombs
that were made for love but are now at war
with murder replacing mother love.

I prayed the rosary today,
for families to raise good children
that love and respect each other
and love the neighbor as themselves.

I prayed the rosary today,
for all those in need
of any prayers at all
that God would keep then in His care.

I prayed the rosary today,
for leaders to make wise decisions
decisions that bring peace and harmony
to all the peoples of the land.

I prayed the rosary today,
that people all over the universe
would turn to God and pray
through all the situations in their lives.

I prayed the rosary today.

Musing at Dusk

(Free Verse)

Perched on the back porch,
Pondering God's nature and wonderful world,
How his love is like a torch
Which lights up my life.

Fireflies flit about to and fro
As dusk settles in on daylight,
Looking for darkness to settle more
Adding beauty to the dark night.

Sun slips silently beyond the horizon so slow
This leaves the earth in eerie darkness,
Until the sun rises in the early morning glow,
When birds awaken and bees buzz about.

I think about daylight which awakens the earth
And the business of the work day ahead
People going to work so they can see their worth
Thanking God for another wonderful day.

Criticism

(Adage)

Stinging criticism seemingly
Damages the soul but diligent prayers
Dispels the venom of a caustic tongue
Thereby leaving the detractors in disarray.

My Delight

(Free Verse)

To praise you Lord is my delight.
Sometimes I think you're out of sight
Your presence in my life, dear Lord
deserves all the praise I can afford.

Day or night you keep me in sight
Help me always to do the right
Be with me on my journey to you
I know that you love me too.

Let not my feet stumble from you afar,
lest I falter and my life I'd mar.
Keep me on the narrow path,
lest I fall and feel your wrath.

The Dance

(Blank Verse)

Make your own sweet music
Dance to your own tune
The steps may not always fit
To the tune you employ.

But as you practice each day
The tones become refined
Making the music fit you
As you dance to your tune.

Others may not understand
The notes of your own song
Since it is your sweet song
No one needs to dance to it.

Dancing to your own tune
Frees you to grow and thrive
Into that person you want to be
Freeing the self to fly free.

Allegany Arts

Speaking the Truth

(Rondelet)

Speaking the truth
Is dangerous and quite risky.
Speaking the truth
You lose friends and acquaintances
Because they fail to understand
That speaking truth is God's command
Speaking the truth.

Speaking the truth
Is not always looked at as good.
Speaking the truth
Will make other people shun you
Although the best route to follow
It can leave some friendships shallow
Speaking the truth.

Be Like

(Free Verse)

Be like the poet who writes
Lines to a special poem in rhyme
Or like a miner seeking pure gold
In forbidden places in olden times.

Be like a gigantic sturdy oak tree
Rooted by the side of a running stream
Or a galloping ebon stallion
With mane streaming like a dream.

Be like a diamond set in a diadem
There is perched on one's head
Or like a person of wisdom
Who knows life's secret and lead

Allegany Arts

Watch your Words

(Free Verse)

Sometimes we think certain words
Especially words of ridicule
Will makes us look cool
But really makes us fools.

Words can heal the soul
Or words can main and kill
Careful of the words you speak
Let not unkind words from you leak.

Peaceful words give comfort
And will heal a sinking soul
Can fill the soul with gladness
Or fill the soul will distress.

So refrain from searing words
That shrivels up the timid soul
Leaving it in deep despair
Unable by it itself to repair.

Life's Journey

(Free Verse)

As I travel along life's journey
Many folks I have met
But you dear folks
I will ne'er ever forget
You fill my life with so much joy
And that . . . my good folks . . .
Is no empty ploy.

Thanksgiving poem to St. Francis Xavier Parishioners on the occasion of
my Diamond Jubilee 2009

Thank you

Advent: A Special Time

(Free Verse)

Advent, a special time of year
Preparing a safe haven in hearts
Whence the Savior comes without fear.

Contemplating with the Virgin Mary
The timely designated time,
Preparing for our King to make merry.

Hearts must be cleansed and pure
All readied for this great feast
That is fast approaching to be sure.

Advent, a special time of year
Flows through our veins
Year after year making all so clear.

That love came down to warm hearts more
Teaching all to live in peace and love
Until we gather on heaven's shore.

Allegany Arts

Racism

(Free Verse)

Racism is a taboo word
Many do not admit it still exists
Some act as if it's a word they'd never heard
Many would not want to resist.

Racism hangs over America like glue
Trying to shake it off is hard
It makes the heart turn blue
Seeking to break free is gooey . . . like lard.

Racism fills you with hate
Pray daily through it and confess
Owning the sin is not too late
God will reward and you bless.

.

Composed at a Workshop on Racism

Our Daily Page

(Free Verse)

Daily we write a page of our life
Each day is a brand new page
These pages will not be lost in strife.

We write our ticket to hell or heaven
Each day we write the things we do
Be it good deeds or mediocre leaven.

We might complain that this is not fair
That we are only human and not responsible
That we are imperfect and need some flair.

But on judgment day out comes the Book
In this book are all the pages we daily wrote
Whether we want to or not we have to look.

We see the pages we wrote each day
Pages of things done or left undone
But God is merciful and will judge us his way.

Repentance can change God's mind
If the pages we wrote are not fine
Jesus is there to forgive the crime.

So be careful what we write
On those pages each day
Cause the road to heaven is quite tight.

Lord, I Need You

(Free Verse)

Lord, I need you today

Come give me comfort
Fill my heart with hope
Fill my heart with faith
Fill my heart with love.

Lord, help me cope today
Life can become burdensome
But with you at my side
All things are possible.

Look not at my imperfections
Fill me with a desire for you
That my sins may not engulf me
And keep me from your grace.

Easter Joy

(Blank Verse)

Easter is a sign of new life
A brand new life of saving grace
Since Christ died to free us from sin
Etching in his heart our saved race
By rising from that stone cold grave.

Joy abound all around the land
Odes of praise and alleluias
Ring out from every church steeple
Your Savior has risen is heard
Sing alleluias to our God.

Songs of jubilation cry out
Taking pleasure in voicing praise
For Christ redeemed our fallen race
Ending our disgrace from the "fall"
Rescuing from damnation . . . all.

Easter

(Free Verse)

Easter, a time of great inner joy
Jesus' God's Son died for our sins
No longer were we steeped in sinful ploy
God's Son washed them all away . . . clean
By the precious shed blood of the Lamb from glory.

Sing songs of thanksgiving and praise
For all of God's grace and mercy
Won for us by the Blood of Jesus Christ raised
On a plank of wood outside the city of Jerusalem
Who rose on the third day setting us all free . . . amazed.

We praise and thank God for Jesus' cross
Who freed us from our bondage to sin
Made us daughters and sons of God, no miss
Able to ascend to the throne of Glory
Where we sing Alleluias in eternal bliss

Allegany Arts

Words

(Anaphora)

Words are mighty powerful utterances
Words can bless
Words can curse
Words can be up-lifting
Words can bring people down
Words can make you feel beautiful
Words can make you feel handsome
Words can sooth the spirit
Words can calm the soul
Words can start a war
Words can bring peace
Words, words, powerful words
Words help us to communicate
Words make the world go round
WORD of God became flesh to redeem humankind
Words, in prayer, connect us to Father, Son and Spirit.

Late Airplanes

(Free Verse)

Late airplanes are really opportunities . . .
They tend to test one's patience to endure
Things that are not to our taste or nature.

Late planes are really opportunities
To meet nice people from other cultures
And form new friendships that will surely endure.

Late planes are really opportunities
To allow time to think and meditate
With time to formulate and to create.

Mindlessness

(Blank Verse)

Because we do not take time
to ponder, meditate and reflect on
important matters and not so important matters,
laxity creeps into our lives.

We have the tendency to say and
do foolish and ugly things
as we encounter each other daily . . .
Unthinkingly.

We forget that we are kindred,
one to the other, sisters and brothers, all
created by the same God, our Father
so let's be kind . . . one to the other.

Mindlessness is not the Christian way,
refrain from the slip of the tongue
as we travel on the journey home.
Time is short . . . waste not a minute.

Trees

(Blank Verse)

Trees are so wonderfully useful
They give us shade
Provide wood for homes
Help to prevent erosion
Provides us with food to eat
Helps freshen the atmosphere
Gives stability to the earth
They even shelter us
From prying eyes
Trees . . .
Our friends
Let's take care of them.

Just thinking about the usefulness of trees and how we take so much for granted.

Patience

(Blank Verse)

Patience
Is learned by waiting
Fretting and pining gets us nowhere
Mothers wait nine months
For the birth of a child
Hospital waiting
Brings relief.

Waiting in check-out lines
Helps one to think
There is some merit in waiting
We waited for Jesus
For thousands of years
The best wait is
Waiting for heaven.

In heaven
There is no more waiting.
Ultimately
Our waiting is rewarded.
We receive our just reward
Just because
We were patient.

Forgive Us

(Senryu)

Forgive us, O Lord
For killing your only Son
On that Friday noon.

How can we make up
For that dastardly action
Perpetrated there?

By righteous pure lives,
Love and care for each other
As our family.

Never maligning
Neighbors . . . sisters or brothers
Living in true peace.

Forgive us, O Lord
For killing your only Son
On a Friday noon.

Three Crosses On A Hill

(Couplets)

Three crosses stood on a craggy hill
The hush is so brutally still, still
A cross to some always spells of doom
On that Good Friday it dispelled gloom.

God's Son, Jesus was nailed to one tree
Lifted high for everyone could see.
Mercy and grace became friends that day
Salvation had to be won this way.

Come down from that cross some mocked with scorn
As he hung rejected and forlorn.
Let us see your grand miracles now
Come down from that cross and take a bow.

Three hours of suffering and pain
Seemed as if nothing good would be gained
By Jesus staying on that rough cross
While below, dice for his clothes are tossed.

Something else was happening for free
Salvation was won from that ole tree.
Life freely given for souls, his way
Redemption was won on this blessed day.

Father James Hector Joubert, SS

(Free Verse)

Joubert . . . a faithful friend and mentor
With Mary Lange, forged a brand new path
Peopling the church with a new religious center.

Helped founded the Oblates Sisters, a fact
Thirty-two years before slavery ended
What a bold and dangerous act!

Joubert allowed the Holy Spirit to use him
Being unafraid of the local naysayer
But embraced the Sisters and loved them.

Now he's crown with glory in heaven to the end
Praying and watching over us his daughters
Hand in hand with Mary Lange his fast friend.

OBLATE SISTERS ... 180 YEARS

(Free Verse)

180 years is a very long time,
Many years for the Lord well spent
Using all the graces God sent.

Times were hard but not insurmountable
Because God the Father had our back
Giving Oblates all that they lacked.

180 years spent in God's vineyard
Trusting in Divine Providence's will
Aware that God would always fill the till.

Racial hatred or prejudice did not prevail
Hands very powerful held Oblates' hands,
Sending them to labor in foreign lands.

Grateful are Oblates all
For God's guidance and forbearance
Never leaving Oblates side, giving deliverance.

OSP

Drip, Drip, Drip

(Free Verse)

Drip, drip, drip
Money going down the drain
Like down-pouring rain.

Drip, drip, drip
Faucet left unattended
As water careens
Down the drain.

Drip, drip, drip
All because we do not screw
That little knob.

Drip, drip, drip
Money down the drain
Like falling rain.

Drip, drip, drip
Be conscious
Of money saved from the drip
After taking a little sip.

So stop that drip, drip, drip.

Marshmallow Clouds

(Haiku)

Soft marshmallow clouds
Fluffy white moves placidly
Like smooth whipped white cream.

Unmindful of jets
Gliding across their vast space
Happy just to be.

Amazing Grace

(Acrostic)

Amazing grace that set me free
Making me a child of the king
Always allowing me to be free for thee
Zeroing in on the great mercy it brings
Inciting me to grow daily to be me
Never putting me down, allowing me to sing
Glory to the amazing love and mercy of thee.

Glory and praise outpours from me as I sing,
Remembering the love you give each day for me to see
Amazing grace is mine each day with zing
Coaxing me to live as a child of the Sacred Tree.
Etching in my heart that love gleaned for me.

Dad

(Blank Verse)

Dad was strong
And tender.
Taught important life lessons.
Showed respect to everyone.
A model
Of incredible strength.

A loving father
Who recognized
In family . . . everyone is special
And deserves
To be your own person
And loved
On one's own merit.

Depression

(Free Verse)

Depression visits every heart
Go to God, give not stress a start
We must not let it touch the soul
If not your very soul will fold.

Depression sneaks into your mind
Tells you that no peace you'll find
Seek help to aid you through this test
Thus taking steps to find some rest.

Depression should not bring us shame
Do not lament or assume blame
Prayer and knowledge . . . helps the stress,
Brings some relief and God we can bless.

If Only

(Free Verse)

If only, is a cliché,
That we should never say.
When we look back at life
When there is some strife.

Regretting what life has sent
Not making good use of the present
We spend a lifetime saying, if only.
That word can make us so lonely.

We waste much time on these two words
These two words should never be heard.
All things are possible with the Lord
With God nothing is impossible or hard.

If only, disappears into the night
Like a bolt of flashing light
If we look at life with faith we gain relief
We put God in place of, if only, by our belief.

Into Each Life

(Free Verse)

God loves us so very much
He wants us to be happy as such
Thanking God is always the right way
For it gives us such great joy to obey.

Thank you God for your good gifts
Wrapped daily in different kinds of bags
Making us grateful each passing day
Not knowing your surprises today.

Forgive

(Blank Verse)

When others think you have committed
an offense against them—
Forgive.

When you are falsely accused by your companions
And only you and God know the answer—
Forgive.

When others misjudge, disrespect you or your actions—
Forgive.

When you have done your very best and still that's not enough –
Forgive.

When others make fun of you because of your infirmities—
Forgive.

Harbor no bitterness for this kills the spirit—
Forgive.

Many are ignorant of their hurtful talk and attitudes—
Forgive.

God sees our sins and failings and forgives us each time we sin –
Forgive.

We become like God when we ignore the sins of our neighbors –
Forgive.

Jesus Our Light

(Free Verse)

God gave us his best
We need not worry about the rest
He sent Jesus to take the test.

To Calvary Jesus went
To claim the prize God sent
The cross for three hours he spent.

Love died on that tree
Just to set us free
Yes. He dies for you and for me.

How marvelous is God's love
Caring for us like a hovering dove
Looking down on us from above.

Thank you, God, for giving us Jesus
Please thank him for us
As we try to love him thus.

Thank you, Jesus, our light
Keep us in your sight
Out from dark of night.

Little Pine Tree

(Haiku/Senryu)

A little pine tree
straight and tall in the bright sun
Enjoying its world.

One day men with saws
And axes came to their home
Seeking Christmas trees.

Unknown to the trees,
The purpose of such a tree
But they would soon see.

Trees were bounded fast
Thrown in a huge truck all crammed
without air to breathe.

Folks shook our branches
Finding the best of the pines
As their Christmas tree.

Lights and colored balls
Adorned my green outstretched arms
To welcome Christmas.

A blessed Christmas
All . . . with joy, peace much love
And Joyous New Year!

Introspection

(Adage)

Introspection leads to an encounter
With the conscious which leads to
Knowledge of one's inner chamber that
Ultimately seeks the Alpha and the Omega
Eventually.

Keeping Others In Their Sins

(Free Verse)

We keep others in their sins
When we broadcast their faults . . . they can't win
God alone knows our heart and its intent
God alone needs us to acknowledge shortcomings and repent.

Charity dictates that we check not our neighbor
Leave the chastising to God who shows no favor.
If we wish to be holy, abide by God's laws
He alone knows we all have plenty of flaws.

Take care of your own sins and leave others to God.
God is the only judge and will spare or not spare the rod.
Let us zip our lips about the faults of one another
And try to raise up our sister and our brother.

Lord, I Need You

(Free Verse)

Lord, I need you today
Come give me comfort
Fill my heart with hope
Fill my heart with faith
Fill my heart with love.

Lord, help me cope today
Life can become burdensome
But with you at my side
All things are possible.

Look not at my imperfections
Fill me with a desire for you
That my sins may not engulf me
And keep me from your grace.

Lord, I Am Available

(Free Verse)

Lord, I am available to you right now
Use me Lord, as you know how.
My life is in your hands God, to mold
So take my hand and lead me to the fold.

Sometimes I might balk at your voice
Asking me to work in this world of your choice
But you are the Potter and I only the clay.
Use me Lord and mold me in your way.

People and things might lead me astray
But you Lord, have power to lead me your way
Situation may not be to my liking
And someone may rule and I go hiking.

You Lord, pull me back from doing mean things
Allow me to sit, listen and keep me under your wings
Lord, make me available to you
Not my will but your will all the way through.

I am available to you, so use me
Use me like an earthen jar for Thee
Fashion and mold me into another you
Let me live not for me but you live in me too.

Lord of Love

(Blank Verse)

Lord of love and infinite goodness
Look with compassion on your children today
Who are reeling under catastrophic conditions
In the land of their beloved country, Haiti.

Embrace and care for them in this time of strife
Continue to give them all the help they need
You know their hearts and souls
Give them your compassion and love.

Forgive their imperfections and transgressions
Lord, guide then in your way
Knowing that you are the giver of all gifts
Thank you for sending humanitarian assistance.

Teach them to learn to lean on you alone
That you will comfort then always
Let not their consciences chide them
Let them know that you love all your children.

Lord You Are Appreciated

(Blank Verse)

Lord, I appreciate your loving care of me
Often I do not show you how much I love you
No one loves me like you do
You died for me, yes, just for me
If I was the only person on this earth
You would have still died for me.

I know this because no matter my sinfulness
You still loved me, yes me!
I am humbled by this and want to tell you so
Help me to love you in the same way you love me
Help me Jesus, for without you I would fall.

Allegany Arts

Bridge Crossing

(Blank Verse)

Life is like crossing a bridge.
We walk from one side to the other.

But what is under the bridge?
That's life . . . the things we see,
and the things unseen under the bridge.

We must focus on the known
and leave the unknown to the Lord.

Love is Entanglement

(Blank Verse)

Love is entanglement with the Divine
Nothing in the world will matter
While embracing the beloved
No goods, money, or fame satisfies
As the soul yearns for the embrace of the Divine
This yearning for the Divine is unquenchable.

We need the Lord like we need a drink of water
Since no one can live without it
Our soul will dry up like the desert
Longing for the entanglement with the Divine
As we gain this nearness to our God
Life is a bearable foe . . . we have found our soul.

On Life's Journey

(Rondelet)

On life's journey
We might find ruts in the road
On life's journey
We might run into enemies
Who would entrap us with fool's gold?
We win if God is our stronghold
On life's journey.

On life's journey
Our eyes must be on saving grace
On life's journey
We forge a new friendship with the Lord
Remembering our steadfast goal
Remaining in the Word and fold
On life's journey.

On life's journey
Falter not over small stumbling blocks
On life's journey
Hard work will yield great piece of mind
So balk not at stumbling strife
God will give us eternal life
On life's journey.

Opportunity

(Blank Verse)

Opportunity, it is said, knocks only once
But with God this is not so,
Opportunity, with God, knocks every day.

Each day opportunity knocks
So that we have the opportunity
To be reclaimed every day.

Opportunity knocks daily
With the almighty, opportunity
Knocks, giving us the opportunity
To begin a brand new day, day after day.

Harriet Tubman

A Woman Who Stirred the Waters

(Free Verse)

Harriet Tubman did not mind stirring the waters
Or even putting her life at risk for others.
A woman of courage and deep conviction
Tramping under foot death for her sisters and brothers.

Totally committed to the task of the Head-Master,
Three hundred times . . . running from South to North
North to South just to set her kin folks free
She paid no mind to empty threats, but bravely set forth.

Harriet stirred the waters like John the Baptist of old
Who eventually lost his head . . . but lived a life of quality.
Harriet Tubman was totally committed to the cause
The cause of total freedom, justice and equality.

This dedication should spur us on to give no pause
To the task of the Head-Master
Who's work we're employed
As we work for our just reward in the here-after.

Harriet Tubman is our super, super hero
Whose life gives us courage to walk the walk each day
Heeding Jesus' command, to care for sheep and lambs
And heaven you'll surly find, seeking God's way.

So, let us stir the waters daily in our busy world
Striving diligently for that peace, only a merciful God can give
Ministering to God's children lest they go astray
As we give good examples by the way we live.

Stir the waters like Harriet and commit to service
Thanking God for the ability to be sacrifice.

Patience

(Free Verse)

Patience
Is learned by waiting
Fretting and pining gets us nowhere
Mothers wait nine months
For the birth of a child
Hospital waiting
Brings relief.

Waiting in check-out lines
Helps one to think
There is some merit in waiting
We waited for Jesus
For thousands of years
The best wait is
Waiting for heaven.

In heaven
There is no more waiting.
Ultimately
Our waiting is rewarded.
We receive our just reward
Just because,
We were patient.

Patsy ... My Good Friend

(Free Verse)

One of my friends went to God the other day
My heart was broken I must say
Girlfriends we were from the ninth grade
A good friend like in heaven was made.

Played soft and basketball together
A great player . . . met our expectation each gathering
Never a spoiled sport always up-beat
Gee, she really could take the coaches' heat.

Always had positive things to say
To her all your troubles you could bring and stay
God gave her a heavy cross later in life, you see
Contracted cancer and had to learn to just be.

We will miss her wit and winning smile
So selfless would treat you gentle like a child
Speaking softly as she wove you a tale
Of something of hers that had to be said.

Be at rest my dear friend and boon
Betty Ann, Agnes and I'll be with you soon
Save a good place for us at the Welcoming Table.
No more talk about them ole' oyster tales.

Happy were the times we had together
To banter about school days and other matters
Remembering, Eva, Mary Sam, Edward, Moses and me.
And all that which had filled us with glee.

Prince of Peace

(Free Verse)

Prince of peace
Make all wars cease
Let love increase.

Send your peaceful dove
To fill all hearts with love
Coming from heaven above.

Permit us not to mope
Help your friends cope
Give us great hope.

You are always near
Aiding us in our fear
Making all crystal clear.

Prince of peace
Make all wars cease
Let love increase.

Allegany Arts

Redemptive Love

(Senryu)

Jesus came to earth
as a babe in a manger
warmed by animals.

To save human kind,
from the fall in the garden,
many years ago.

Christmas is our gift,
from God our loving Father,
making us his heirs.

It is a time to
believe and heed the Good News,
that Jesus is Lord.

The Christmas season
is really for us adults
and not for children.

But in the Christmas
Season all become children
of Redemptive Love.

Satiated

(Adage)

Being satiated is a myth
There will always be a craving in the heart
This drives us toward that which tries to
Satisfy our deeper longing for truth and love.
Elusion surrounds those who seek
Worldly grandeur and satisfaction.
God is the only one who can
Satiate our thirst.

Allegany Arts

Speech

(Blank Verse)

Speech couched in semantics
Gives the impression of knowledge
Makes the speaker incoherent to the observer
Feigning that which is incorrigible and trite.

Clarity of speech benefits both
The speaker and hearer to give not only
Appearances but truth and sincerity.

Take It to the Lord

(Blank Verse)

When people say mean and unflattering things about you
Take it to the Lord in prayer.
When you have done your very best and feel unblessed
Take it to the Lord in prayer.

When your friends disappoint you
Take it to the Lord in prayer.
When dreams are shattered by well meaning people
Take it to the Lord in prayer.

When you've done your best and people think you are all that
Take it to the Lord in prayer.
When you have done your best and get stabbed in the back
Take it to the Lord in prayer.

When your confidence is compromised
Take it to the Lord in prayer.
When misunderstood, gossiped about and others shun you
Take it to the Lord in prayer.

When your work is tampered with and destroyed
Take it to the Lord in prayer.
When your gifts and talents are not appreciated
Take it to the Lord in prayer.

Thank you, Lord

(Blank Verse)

Thank you, Lord for waking me this day
How can I thank you for this grace
You are so good to your children
For you are the source of all life-forces.

Lord, you are our beginning and ultimate end
To you we go when in dire need.
Teach us to love each other even when we balk,
No one can care for us like you can.

You are the only person we can lean on
And trust that you will give us relief
There is none like you Lord, none like you
Your Son laid down His life for us all.

Never allow us to take your love for granted
Give us strength to live by your laws.
Show us how to love each other as we should
By following your example of selflessness.

Be our guide as we take up our cross daily
As we imitate the life and legacy of Jesus
Who laid down His life for us on Calvary.
We thank you for the gift of Jesus, your Son.

Thanksgiving

(Free Verse)

Every day is a day of Thanksgiving.
It's a time of righteous living
Thanking God for His bountiful blessings.
Acknowledging God's love and confessing
That all things are given from above
Sent to us from heaven with love.

There are no accidents in life
Only planned events to help in strife.
Many gifts are wrapped in some pain
If accepted in God's light yield gain.
Thanking God for life's woes, love and joy
Will produce a fruitful life to enjoy.

Gratitude

(Anaphora)

Gratitude is relying on God for all things
Gratitude is trusting God in all situations
Gratitude is being thankful for life
Gratitude is willing to give all to God
Gratitude sustains us in our daily lives
Gratitude is being honest with God
Gratitude allows us to walk with Jesus daily
Gratitude allows God to use us at will
Gratitude leads us to become wisdom people
Gratitude relies on the Providence of God
Gratitude shows love at all time
Gratitude fills our hearts with joy
Gratitude makes us forgiving people
Gratitude makes us count our many blessings
Gratitude makes us use our gifts for God
Gratitude will lead eventually to heaven.

Today

(Anaphora)

Today is all I have
Today is all that is promised
Today is mine to make holy
Today is the only sure day
Today is not a promise of tomorrow
Today is God's gift to me
Today is my day, all mine
Today is the day to get things right
Today is my blessing day
Today is all mine, I must live it well.

Allegany Arts

Winter

(Free Verse)

Winter is not my time of year
Spring, Summer and Fall are for me unique
Winter has its own mystery I fear
Like each snow flake with its own mystique.

Winter does have its perks to be sure
It clears the air of germs and all
Making the earths atmosphere pure
Clearing the air for a beautiful Spring and Fall.

Winter cautions you to be careful in snow.
It can't help you if you slip on its icy floor
But you must see how it gives us a great show
Blanketing the earth with snow . . . watering earth's core.

Winter makes us stop, prepare and detect
What God wants us to do for the journey home aright.
Putting on the armor of salvation and reflect,
Only God's blessings are wrapped up in pure white.

Winter gives us a head-up for what's coming next.
If we heed the signs of the time life will be alright.
The Bible is the sign with the right text
We don't want to slip and slide and lose the fight.

God Hears Me When I Pray

(Free Verse)

God hears me when I pray.
Sometimes we need to holler our say,
I've got to get God's attention it seems.
Even when I am low in my own esteem.

God hears me when I pray
Even when I go astray.
No matter my situation in life
No matter the amount of strife.

God hears me when I pray
Although flat on my back I lay.
When people are mean and unkind to me
To my gracious God I flee.

God hears me when I pray
I just have to get out of the way.
Nothing is too great for my God
Though sometimes God spares not the rod.

God hears me when I pray
If nearby his side I stay,
And listen to his voice
He always gives me a choice.

God hears me when I pray.

Writing

(Free Verse)

Writing takes time
To think and to meditate
To figure out what type
Of poetry or form of writing to create.

Sometimes writing is forced
Thinking words will flow
Simply by willing or coercion
Willing the mind to bestow.

Writing will come when at ease
Flowing from the inner spirit
Allowing the mind to cruise
To the place where the writing spirit flit.

Stability

(Free Verse)

Stability in life depends not solely on us
But comes from a deep trust
In the inscrutable love of God
Who loves us, even in our sinful trod.

Relying on self for all our needs
Is like planting opened seeds.
God is the planter, we the crops
That must be watered with divine rain drops.

God is our sure anchor now
That helps us sail in life somehow
Making us see though His eyes
That to Him all are tied.

Humans

(Free Verse)

We humans think we are all that
Forgetting that we are all creatures
Made in God's image is a fact
No one can change one's feature.

We look with disdain on our neighbor
Because they do not look like us
Not knowing that we are here by God's favor
To love and to serve Him without fuss.

Not one color can we change on others
Or nose or lips remake in this world or the next
God alone has power to create
We need to bow to God's laws in the Biblical text.

God command us to love our sisters and brothers
No matter the color of the skin or nationality
Hair texture or length of the nose
All must be loved because we are all kin in reality.

Be Like

(Free Verse)

Be like the poet who writes
Lines to a special poem in rhyme
Or like a miner seeking pure gold
In forbidden places in olden times.

Be like a gigantic sturdy oak tree
Rooted by the side of a running stream
Or a galloping ebon stallion
With mane streaming as in a dream.

Be like a diamond set in a diadem
That is perched on ones head
Or like a person of wisdom
Who knows life's secret and lead.

Cheaters

(Blank Verse)

People who cheat
and connive
are not pleasing
to God.

They will do anything
to get their own way
lie, cheat or steal
just about anything.

Sometimes even ruin
the good names of others
just to get their way
and please self.

There is a special place
in the nether world
for such a one as this
if left to falter.

Because we serve
a merciful God
repentance can save
anyone who asks.

For We Are Family

(Free Verse)

Family gathering are fun times
But are sad when someone dies
Although sad, it shows concern that binds
When all come to relieve sorrowful stress
For we are Family.

Family gather after funeral rites
To eat and reconnect anew
Binding family members together tight
In love through unity in grief
For we are Family.

Children meet cousins now
Exchanging e-mails and such
Connecting through sorrow somehow
Knowing that the bonding must survive.
For we are Family.

Leadership Is About Love

(Chain)

Leadership is a call to service
Service implies no favoritism
Favoritism leads to bad discord
Discord leads to blatant anarchy
Anarchy leads to sly rebellion
Rebellion leads to untimely war
War wounds the spirit, causing division
Division leads to moral breakdown
Breakdown leads to mental distraction
Distraction to annihilation
Annihilation destroys our peace
Peace is necessary for service
Service implies dedicated love
Love is what leadership is about.

Worry Not

(Acrostic)

Worry is a waste of time
Often it is about nothing we can change
Rehashing what could or should have been
Reviewing that for which we have no control
Yet, yearning for some peace of mind.

Nothing is served by fretting
Our time must be spent in a positive mood
Taking our worries to God, our Helper.

Life

(Free Verse)

Life has its ups and downs
It is not like a clown
Making jokes in the park
It's not about looking for a lark.

Life is a serious journey
Neighbors on the journey will be funny
Others on the way will be stern
Through it all . . . for God's love, you will yearn.

Life is a school that teaches.
Its lessons are hard to breach
Sometimes the lessons are sweet
If we allow God to fashion or treat.

Life's journey has an end
Happy the one who knows to attend
To all that God sends each day
For through it all, God will make a way.

Upon that Tree

(Free Verse)

To see you Jesus upon that tree
There was no solace for me
I sit in my comfortable room
Too lazy to lift a little broom.

Knowing how you loved me thus
Still I mope and pout as I fuss
Coping was your great skill
Yet a pain and I . . . seek a pill.

Calvary was no child's play
Want to have everything my way
Help me Jesus to carry my tiny cross
When hard situations I would toss.

Lead me to that sad hillside each day
Never let me have my way or my say
Knowing that you are with me to stay
As long as I walk the narrow way.

Lord You Promised

(Anaphora)

Lord you promised . . .

To give us what we need
To always be faithful
To not leave us orphans
To always abide with us
To be our guide in troubled times
To be our friend
To be our counselor
To be a comforter
To be our parent
To love us unconditionally
To take us to heaven if we serve you.

Prayer Has No Limit

(Anaphora)

Prayers have no limit with God
Pray to God with abandonment
Pray to God to answer all prayers
Prayer is all we need to connect to God.

Pray when all seems hopeless
Pray when all goes well
Pray for any and all things
Prayer will get you anything.

Prayer will get God's attention
Prayer is the panacea for all things
Prayers make God take note of everything we ask.
Prayers will get you to heaven.

Nature At It's Best

(Free Verse)

We see God in all of nature.
It is God, seen at God's very best
Sharing beauty for the future
Giving us night so we could rest.

Nature has not one earthly care
Prodding along at it's own pace
Basking in God's power to share
Sharing in the Almighty's grace.

Humans are lucky, you can see
Thanking you everyday for you
Because God, we can talk to thee
Praising you for all blessings too.

So we thank you for earth so green
For animals that roam so free.
And for all the beauty we glean
Like hearing birds in an old oak tree.

Thank you for the flowers that bloom
For children playing in the field
And for Spring that leaves way too soon
For those who labor for their yield.

There is no other God but thee
Who treats us so well and so free.

Rage in the World

((Free Verse)

Lord this world is full of unbridle raging rage
Use your divine power to give us your peace
Hatred and carnage keep us all in locked cages
Lord, let rage decrease and peace increase.

Nations and Cities all over this world gone wrong
There's killing and looting all for power and greed
Love of neighbor . . . thoughts of the past . . . all gone
Send down your angels to help us . . . hear our need.

Women, children and young boys raped and killed
Many misplaced all for the sake of nationhood
Pillages of town, villages, and no more farms to till
Starvation is the norm in the neighborhood.

No one safe in this world of human torches
Bombs flying, the earth weeping for respect
People dying in a senseless stance of reproaches
No one's safe from the ravage of rage we detect.

Throw Away Society

(Anaphora)

We throw away paper cups and plates
We throw away out of style clothing
We throw array nearly new shoes
We throw away our children
We throw away our friends
We throw away our culture
We throw away our parents
We throw away anything that curbs our freedom
We throw away our marriages by divorces
We throw away our allegiance to God
We, if we are not careful, will throw away our souls.
We must resist the urge of being a throw away society.

The Ethiopian Eunuch

(Acrostic)

Ebon of skin so handsome and strong
The Ethiopian Eunuch rode meditatively along
Hovering over scripture passages
In his chariot, reading . . . musing . . . alone
Of Isaiah who wrote sacred messages
Pillar of the Candace
Influential and true to his race
Accounting to the most high God
Noting Gods love of us all who sometimes spare the rod.

Evaluating his life of service
Untiring and giving servant
Never thinking of the self
Undying love of his ministry
Counting on God who is infinity
Honoring God by his call to proclaim the Word made Flesh for
    all eternity.

Silence

(Adage)

Silence keeps us in touch with us
Listening for God requires peace
Busy lives need a noise release
to hear answers without ruckus.

Our Priests

(Acrostic)

Outstanding champions of God on every occasion,
Using one's priestly faculty to minister to all folks and
Ready at a moment's notice . . . to be of service.

Priests according to the order of Melchizedek,
Respectful of all life, from conception to death.
Integrity of mind and spirit . . . leaning always on God,
Ever ready to be missionaries for Christ's Church.
Satisfied with the priestly life chosen with the ability
To transform wine into Christ's Body daily and impart
Solace at the end of life's journey . . . is a bridge to God.

Forgiveness

(Couplet)

God loves us when we seek true forgiveness
If we forgive, God will relent and bless.

Forgiveness is no easy task to do
God will forgive you and reward you too.

Unforgiveness will take our souls to hell
We must forgive or our souls we will sell.

If you forgive, God will forget your sins
And your soul'll be set for heaven to win.

Silence Calms the Soul

(Sonnet)

Silence calms the searching and wayward soul
It melds us with the heavenly Maker
Giving us time for reflection to mold
Willing souls for union with the Master.

Silence makes us look deeper with great awe
Down into our inner most recesses,
Allows other to see us as we are,
Calling us to continuous progress.

Silence takes us to the feet of our God
Who view us a we really are each day
Thus forgiving sins and sparing the rod
Pondering our humanness as we pray

Silence is God's way of refining us
Making us all truly His children thus.

Serving God

(Free Verse)

God showers us with blessings each day
With his immutable love and grace
As I go about duty or play
God is there to talk or embrace.

God must not be taken for granted
For his giving ways and all
But we need to work where planted
Lest we stumble and fall.

Loving God is not that hard
When we see all God's goodness to us
Sustaining us . . . being our rear guard
As we serve God daily without fuss.

Days of The Week

(Acrostic)

Sunday

Saving grace and restful peace
Under Gods umbrella
Needing time to worship and praise
Deeply in heart's recess
Adoring the Godhead who made us
Yielding to peace and tranquility.

Monday

Mourning that Monday is here already
Out and up from bed
Needing to earn one's keep
Dealing with other folks . . .
Attending to basic demands
Year after year . . . But we thank God for Mondays.

Tuesday

Trudging to work day two
Using much energy too
Eeeking out another workday
Sorting out precious time
Doing what is expected
Assured of pay at the end of the week
Yearning for rest and the colored TV.

Wednesday

Where has the week gone?
Everything seems to perk up
Day going too quickly
Noon here and work half done
Endurance is the key to
Satisfaction for a God-given
Day to say thank you, Lord
Always for sunshine or rain and
You look forward to tomorrow.

Thursday

Thanksgiving to God for a
Heavenly peaceful sleep
Under the guidance
Radiant canopy of
Sun streaming through slats
Drowning our night's gloom
As daylight clamors vigorously
Yearning for another day of the Son.

Friday

Fervent aspirations
Remembering the price paid when
I was redeemed on that dark
Day on a Hill called Calvary
Aching to atone for
Years of neglect of my God.

Saturday

Situated between Friday and Sunday
Abandoned it seemed
To mediocrity
Uniting the profane and sacred
Raising awareness of the needs of
Duty to sustain stability
And access to malls, games and TV
Yelling for some tranquility.

Allegany Arts

Nurses

(Free Verse)

Nurses are Angels sent by God.
Sent to work in God's place
To heal and to sooth by His grace.

Nurses are Angels sent by God.
They place others above themselves and stand tall
As they minister with love to all.

Nurses are Angels sent by God.
Day after day they serve us well
Regardless of inclement weather or spell.

Nurses are Angels sent by God.
They provide us with love
Provided by our God from above.

Nurses are Angels sent by God.

Choices

(Free verse)

Choices are made daily,
Some good and some bad.
Take care how you rally
Around the choices you make today.

Choose wisely your daily choices,
For each choice that's wisely made
Brings you closer to heavenly voices
As we prepare for the journey.

If you pay choices no heed
We might think there's no necessity
To pay attention to our daily need
To formulate good choices in life.

Right choices keeps us from a stumble
And will bring us heavenly blessings
If each day we do not gamble
With the wisdom God gives us each day.

Soothing Music

(Blank Verse)

Birds singing sweetly outside my window
Helped to sooth the pain I felt.
This thought brought to mind a bible verse,
"If God takes care of the birds of the air
Surely he will take care of me."

Jesus died for me and not for birds
So I feel safe when all's not well
Bright is the day and calm is the night
For I know God is at my side.

Earth may shake and rivers may swell
Nor will evil spirits upset me.
God is with me as with the birds
And all of nature who know God's name.

Trouble At the Water Hole

(Bland Verse)

All is not well at the water hole right now
Rumors are flying that there's trouble down the road in DC.

All is not well at the water hole right now
We cannot agree if we are together right now.

All is not well at the water hole right now
Democrats and Republicans are banded against each other.

All is not well at the water hole right now
Republicans want all the concession . . . Will give nothing up.

All is not well at the water hole right now
Democrats bending over backwards to agree.

All is not well at the water hole right now
Prayers are offered up for the Leader of the Nation.

All is not well at the water hole right now
We must come to some agreement for the good of the whole.

All is not well at the water hole right now
Only God can get us out of the mess we're in.

All is not well at the water hole right now.

Blessings

(Free Verse)

There are blessings in illness
It slows you down to help you ponder life.
You see ordinary things as miracles not strife.
The eyes of the mind opens as if seeing a new dress.

You welcome each new day with thanksgiving.
People become dearer and life becomes bearable
Time is precious not to be wasted but valuable
Life is looked at as something fragile and life-giving.

Illness allows one to be genuinely humble
Allowing others to wait on us for a time
Having a thankful spirit . . . refusing to grumble.
While allowing others to dress, feed and make us shine.

Laughter

(Couplet)

Laughter is good for the soul
At least that is what we're told.

Nothing is more soothing to the ears
It tingles the spirit and calms all fears.

Not all laughter calms the spirit
Some can sear the soul and kill it.

Some laughter lulls our souls to sadness
Turning our mirth into madness.

But be not dismayed God is the way
Turning our pain into joy always.

For laughter is God's gift to us
Giving us joy for the journey . . . no fuss.

Christ's Love for Us

(Cascade)

Christ died for saints and sinners too
Yes, Jesus died for me and for you
By hanging alone on that tree
So that we could just be free.

As followers of the Son of God
We pray that God will spare the rod
Lest we forget what Jesus did.
Christ died for saints and sinners too.

Walking the walk each day of life
Saves us from a whole lot of strife
Allowing us to be grateful too
Yes, Jesus dies for me and for you.

Thank you Jesus for the cross
That saved us all from heaven's loss
Buying us back from Satan's glee
By hanging alone on that tree.

Daily we strive to do good deeds
Lovingly sewing good seeds
Seeking to serve the Triune three
So that we could just be free.

PRAISE

(Free Verse)

Let our praise rise
To the Lord for blessings
Each day . . .

As God feeds us
Daily with
His Word and Sacrament,
His way . . .

Praying we draw nearer
To Christ
To stay!

Easter Sunday

(Acrostic)

Easter Sunday, a day to honor Christ
As Savior and as Lord
Standing in our stead
Taking on our sins
Etching in our memory
Redemption's saving grace.

Suddenly like thunder
Under shaking earth
New Life burst asunder
Death is lord no longer.
Alleluias fill the air for
You, Lord Jesus, has Arisen.

Sweet Alleluias

(Senryu)

Sweet Alleluias
Filled the Easter Sunday morning air
Jesus has risen.

Sweet Alleluias
Bring forth peals of joy
Christ has risen.

Sweet Alleluias
Claiming Vic' try over sin
For Christ has risen.

Articulation

(Adages)

I

Mere articulation
Assuages not the heart of Christ
But contrite refutation of sins.

Disasters

II

Catastrophic disasters
Moves the heart to compunction
And empathy allowing the soul
To perform courageous actions.

Fancy Words

(Adages)

III

Flowery words changes
Not an attitude of vengeance
From one who is not contrite.

Atonement

IV

Atonement for wrong-doing
Count as naught without
Retribution.

The Glory of Haiti

(Free Verse)

The glory of Haiti shall reign again
Like the mighty Phoenix from ashes of old
To fly her flag proudly as her legacy she'll regain,
Rising to the height of her glory to unfold.

The glory of Haiti swells in hearts over all the earth
Telling the saga of God's great and mighty power.
Who rules creation for all who acknowledges God's worth,
Of the love and the might that God's mercies shower.

And the glory of the Lord will readily unfold
As we relate the story of God's great power
Which engulfs the soul as the tale is told
Of our God reigning from His heavenly tower.

When we tend to the needs of each sister and brother
Giving loving vibes to those in urgent want and need
Knowing that we are all intertwined with each other
The glory of the Lord will shine on those who feed.

And the glory of the Lord shall shine
When to all we are always kind and ever pure
Bringing humanitarian aid to human kind
Opens the heart of God to all nations we're sure.

The glory of Haiti shall truly reign again
Be placed on the map as her flag joins force
With other nations to barter, trade and gain
World recognition, as in days of old, in due course.

And Haiti shall rise like the mighty Phoenix.

HAM

(Free Verse)

Haiti, beloved country of Mary Lange
We cry out at your devastation today
Thought out the world your crisis bell rang
Countries round the world ran to obey.

Tears of woe and consternation fell quietly
Tearing Port-au Prince to the lowly ground
Building by building careening quickly
Buildings and streets swallowed all around.

How did this tragedy come to be?
A fault under the earth they did say
A point seven on the Richter scale they see
Tearing the earth asunder and nothing can stay.

The dead are buried, mourned and the living to console
Those left behind either above or under rubble
Some under rubble and could be alive, we're told
Workers, using any tool to dig neighbor out of trouble.

The best in humanity was witnessed by its goodness
As all nationalities across the continents to assist
Neighbors helping neighbor without bitterness
All saw the connection of all people and could attest.

Despite those who asked, "Where was God?"
God was there through all of this disorder
Using the elect to help spare His rod
Sent helpers around the globe to restore some order.

Allowing us to see that we are sisters and brothers
All depending on each other to be truly whole
Galvanizing with compassion as children kin to the other

Realizing we are all God's children with immortal souls.

A tragedy, yes, but so much good to insure a noticeable spot.
Countries will rebuild a New Haiti with clarity
Haiti, once ignored, is now on the map at the top
Calling on all who can . . . to lend a helping hand through charity.

Allegany Arts

Sister Magdala Marie Gilbert, OSP is an Oblate Sister of Providence. She has taught many years on the Elementary and High School levels. Sister has been Vocation and Formation Director for her Congregation as well.

She has written numerous articles for the Catholic Review, the Catholic newspaper for the Archdiocese of Baltimore. Each year she writes articles for the "Keep on Teaching" booklet and has articles in the book, "What We Have Seen and Heard," published by the Office of African American Catholic Ministries. She has written a booklet about Mother Mary Lange, OSP called, "One Who Dared, Mary Lange: A Short Portrait," four booklets of poetry "A Tribute to Mother Mary Lange and the Oblate Sisters of Providence," two books of poetry, "Inspirational Musing" and "A Journey In Poetry."